Memories of Grace

Memories of Grace

James Stephen Behrens, OCSO

ACTA
ASSISTING CHRISTIANS TO ACT
PUBLICATIONS

Memories of Grace
Portraits from the Monastery
by James Stephen Behrens, OCSO

Jeffrey Paul Behrens took the name James Stephen when he entered the Monastery of the Holy Spirit in Conyers, Georgia. Fr. Behrens was ordained in the Archdiocese of Newark, New Jersey, where he worked for over twenty years before joining the Trappists.

Edited by Gregory F. Augustine Pierce
Cover design by Tom A. Wright
Typesetting by Desktop Edit Shop, Inc.
Cover photo of cloister walk at Gloucester Cathedral,
    England, by Jean Morman Unsworth
Bible quotes are from the New Revised Standard Version

Published by: ACTA Publications
                Assisting Christians To Act
                4848 N. Clark Street
                Chicago, IL 60640-4711
                773-271-1030

Library of Congress Card Number: 00-111392

ISBN: 0-87946-220-5

Printed in the United States of America

Year: 05 04 03 02 01
Printing: 7 6 5 4 3 2 1

Contents

Dedication

To Mary McCarthy, my sister, who fills my heart with love, my memories with warmth, my life with gratitude.

Introduction

André Dubus, the acclaimed fiction writer who died recently, once said that when he was writing he often had to leave the book and go for a long walk to allow the remainder of the story to somehow find its own voice.

This method applies to much of life. The more we try to force things, the greater our frustration and disappointment. In many ways, it is often best to step back a bit from the busyness of life and allow things to evolve on their own. The verbal portraits offered in this book are examples of the kinds of thoughts that simply come to me as I live and work and pray in the Cistercian monastery here in Conyers, Georgia, preparing myself to make final vows as a Trappist monk. I did not seek these memories, though I confess that I did hope for them and was glad when they arrived. But I had to work to get the words as nearly right as I could, for the writing of these pieces was like giving linguistic form to whispers—passing somethings that arrived as gifts when I least expected them.

I call these portraits "memories of grace." Writing them was like entering into a freely chosen state of forgetfulness that allowed me to remember. They happened whenever the wheels of my daily grind stopped turning long enough for my memory to move itself into a very different gear—not so much a recollection of past events but an awareness of eternal, transcendent truths that I already somehow "knew" in the very fiber of my being.

We all live by such memories. They have a voice, a warm voice, something like the voice I imagine God's to be. It is a voice that speaks to each of us from and through where we have been in our life. In a strange, mystical way, it is a voice that asks us to remember where we are going.

A friend recently challenged me to defend the relevance of contemplative life to today's world, specifically to our fast-paced western society. His was not an angry challenge but a seeking one. He trusts me when I tell him that monastic life has something important to offer those outside the cloister, but I have not been able to articulate for him exactly what that something is.

I do not feel comfortable with the classic distinctions between the contemplative and the active life. Such distinctions blur the common and religious humanity that we all share. I do not have "religious" memories here in the monastery, nor am I filled with "pious" thoughts. I admit that officially sanctioned religious language and symbolism abound in this place as in all other religious institutions, but I think the reality that they point to is present everywhere. Religion has no monopoly on the many ways God is at work and at play in the universe.

We Trappist monks live relatively stable lives, which means simply that we promise to stay put in one place and to be there for each other. Like everyone else, however, we make a living, have our ups and downs, find life at times to be very strange, and sometimes wish a lot of things could be different. Yet we try to do the best we can with the silence, solitude and simplicity that we have chosen by spending our days developing "memories of grace." Learning and teaching how to do that may be what we contemplatives have most to offer others.

So, I invite you to explore some of my "memories of grace," in the hope that you will experience your own.

"Come to me, you who desire me,
and eat your fill of my fruits.
For the memory of me is sweeter
than honey,
and the possession of me sweeter
than the honeycomb."

Sirach 24:19-20

Christopher Street

The memory is simple and returns to me often and unbidden. It is a delight when it comes and lingers for a while. It seems to like, as I do, the quiet of the woods here at the monastery, for that is where it comes to me with such ease.

The memory is of my mom and dad, sitting in their bedroom before going to bed on a warm summer night. We had a large old home on Christopher Street in Montclair, New Jersey. It was a Dutch colonial, and their bedroom was on the second floor. The rest of us, five sons and two daughters and my grandmother—Dad's mom— were scattered comfortably throughout the rest of the house. My twin brother Jimmy and I slept in a small room on the third floor, which had two closets—as if it had been made just for twins. We had our own bathroom at the end of a long hall, and there was a large porcelain tub in there with legs shaped like lions' feet. The toilet was right next to a window that overlooked the back yard, and from that window the Manhattan skyline was visible.

Before going to bed, each of us would stop in and say goodnight to Mom and Dad. We would sit on their bed and chat for a little while. Gram

15

used to stick her head in the door and say a soft goodnight. Dad sat in a large maroon-colored chair by the front window, and Mom sat on the other side of the same window, at Dad's desk. They wore pajamas, and if the night was chilly they wore robes. Mom wore a simple blue robe; Dad's was maroon—the same color as his chair. They smoked back then, though I do not remember the room smelling all that strongly of cigarettes. There was a stronger, sweet smell of talc or perfume. They always had a nightcap before going to bed, usually a light scotch with water.

On summer nights, their window was open unless there was a heavy rain. We could hear cars passing by as we spoke, as well as the occasional soft tread or slap of someone's feet as he or she passed in front of the house. Air conditioning was not common back then, and on a hot summer's night people would take walks in the evening to cool off a bit.

I can see the scene above perfectly, almost 50 years later. With a little effort, I can hear my parents' voices and observe their younger faces. I remember the desk and the ashtray, the pens and the yellow legal pads, an old adding machine. There are a few magazines on the cream-colored radiator cover in front of the window. Mom's and Dad's slippers are under their bed. The lace curtain moves just a bit, toyed with by a light summer breeze. There are lights on in the houses across the street, partially obscured by the large trees that were (and I hope still are) one of the real treasures of Christopher Street. There is a single street lamp, burning bright and around which hundreds of moths swirl and swirl.

> *God's incarnate love comes to me carried by the still, warm breezes of past summer nights, nights when Mom and Dad mysteriously did the "God thing" by living their vows and letting the awesome power of their love seep into and lay claim to the ordinariness of their lives.*

Dad sits with his legs crossed—"man style," and Mom sits in her chair, which is pulled away from the desk and facing me. Her legs are crossed, too, but "ladylike." Her hair is dark, though there are wisps of gray. She keeps it in place with bobby pins.

There are separate dressers on either side of the door. My brothers, Robert and Peter, are long asleep in a room to the left. I can almost touch and feel the things I see: Mom's silver-plated hair brush and mirror set, her jewelry, the little statue of a woman with a fine china dress, stacks of letters and coupons, a few broken rosaries. On Dad's bureau are some papers, a pair of black socks, a shoe horn, his wallet, an open pack of cigarettes and his Zippo lighter.

They smoked non-filtered Pall Malls. Mom would always get a tiny bit of tobacco on her lip when she took a drag on her cigarette. I can see the exact way her hand would go to her lips and gently remove the little piece.

I picture myself in that room, watching them, listening to them, saying a goodnight and kissing them, and then heading on upstairs to bed. I can remember the soft cheek of my mom and the sweet smell of Pond's cold cream as I kissed her. I remember the stubble on Dad's cheek as I kissed him and the faded but still unmistakable smell of the Mennen's Skin Bracer he had splashed on his freshly shaven face that morning.

What did we speak of those many nights? I cannot recall a single conversation in detail. The words escape me, but the sensual memory is strong: the smells, the sights, the colors, the breeze, the distant sound of footsteps of a long-ago night walker. The memory has lasted and seems to grow stronger with each passing year, especially since my dad died a few years ago.

It is strange, even wondrous, when you think about it! We humans are constantly trying to imagine what God is like. Is the divinity male or female, near or far, all knowing, all powerful? We Christians believe that men and women are created in the image and likeness of God. So perhaps learning about God is coextensive with learning about ourselves: how we become who we are, how we remember, and what we remember.

We think of God as some sort of grandiose finished being, and yet our lives, if they are truly human lives at all, become so only through encounters that come scented with Mennen's Skin Bracer and Pond's Cold Cream.

God's incarnate love comes to me carried by the still, warm breezes of past summer nights, nights when Mom and Dad mysteriously did the "God thing" by living their vows and letting the awesome power of their love seep into and lay claim to the ordinariness of their lives. Any one of those nights were like so much leaven, working its magic over the years, stubbornly refusing to be remembered as "inconsequential."

Words

There exist words arranged with such care that they enable us to actually enter the world of the one who wrote them. Even though the author's world might be long ago, it comes back to life and is shared with those who read the words.

I once read a poem printed on a poster encouraging people to read that was affixed to a subway car wall in New York City. It was a poem by a Polish-born writer, Czeslaw Milosz. The words were few, and I cannot remember their order or even the exact phrasing, though I do remember their power and the place to which they brought me as I read them. The poet wrote of a long-ago scene from his youth—a simple walk home on a winter day. He wrote of snow on a fence and a hare running across a field and an old man on the road, visible just out of the corner of the poet's youthful eye and soon to vanish forever. It was a scene once real but long gone, but the words evoked in me the passing mystery of all things.

My heart was heavy that day. I was with my brother, Johnny, and we were riding the subway from a restaurant in Greenwich Village up the West Side of Manhattan. I was to leave for the

Trappist monastery in a few days, and we both knew it was a parting of the ways that was qualitatively different from any previous separation we had experienced. Johnny and I had seen much of each other over the years, and this definitive change in our relationship was painful for us both. We realized that many simple and ordinary activities that we had shared over the years would no longer be possible. Johnny shared my happiness over my long-considered decision to follow the way of life at the Trappist monastery in Conyers, Georgia, far away from Manhattan— both geographically and spiritually. Still, the pain of leaving each other was sharp and deep.

Johnny stood next to me on the crowded subway as I read the poem. We both swayed quietly on the train, aware, I am sure, of the heaviness of heart we both felt. I do not know if Johnny even read the words, though he must have seen them often on his many commutes.

As we rode along, memories of our many lunches together, our rides to Brooklyn to see our cousin Mae, our long chats in the car as I drove him back to his upper West Side apartment late at night imbedded themselves in my soul as surely as the scene from Poland had seared itself into the imagination of Czeslaw Milosz.

The words of the poet made me think of the

love in which we are all immersed that makes us suffer and yet rejoice and moves some of us to write of things that happened long ago in order to redeem them and make them live forever.

> *We parted, carrying within us something new: a sense of the past born with that farewell–a past that birthed a new beginning in our lives.*

On that day, on the corner of 57th Street and Eighth Avenue, my brother hugged me as we said good-bye to each other. He held me close to him as if he wanted to hold and remember that moment. We parted, carrying within us something new: a sense of the past born with that farewell—a past that birthed a new beginning in our lives.

There is a man who used to sing opera aloud on West 57th Street. I saw him each time I went into the city from my parish in Newark. He suffered from what might be considered a disturbed condition, but he did not seem to care what others may have thought of him as they passed him by. He just sang with all his heart, looking up at the skyscrapers all around him. He seemed quite happy to me. He probably took whatever money was offered him for his arias, though I do not recall ever having seen a little tin cup. I only remember seeing him with his hands folded on his chest, his eyes raised to the heavens as he sang.

He was there the day my brother and I parted, and I hope that he is still there today as I write this.

My words will probably never find their way onto the wall of any subway car, but they have found their way into this book. What have I to remember? No hare, no snow, no old man passing. But I have other etchings on my heart: a hug from my brother, the song of a man on a street, a ride uptown, a poem on a subway poster. These things bespeak a mystery that lives through all of us; rides with all of us; enfolds, beckons, moves, loves all of us.

The Gift of Wine and Cheese

Mr. and Mrs. Fisher owned a newspaper store on Watchung Avenue in Montclair, New Jersey, where I grew up. It was a small store, with a soda counter, toys and candies, cigars and cigarettes, school supplies and newspapers and magazines.

The Fishers were Jewish, as I and all the kids knew because they closed the store on days that seemed odd to us. We were used to our own feasts and holidays, but we were just beginning to appreciate the other religious and cultural worlds that people inhabited, even though they lived and worked on the same streets as we did. It was, after all, the 1960s, that decade of budding tolerance for those who are somehow different from ourselves.

I can still hear the sound of the store's screen door that swung open and closed hundreds of times each summer afternoon. "Fisher's" was a favorite hangout for the kids of the neighborhood, and the couple never chased us out. Mr. Fisher was a kind man, short and always neatly dressed. He liked cigars and took great pleasure in nursing a stub for hours, carefully laying it aside in the ashtray he always kept within reach. His wife was a pleasant-looking woman and a great listener. She loved to hear us talk about school and home life, and she was sympathetic (way more than most of our parents were) to the trials and tribulations of growing up in an increasingly crazy world. I do not think that I ever saw her when she was not drying a dish or a glass, or wiping the long linoleum counter and ringing out the cloth after each pass.

The Fishers had one son, who was studying to be a doctor. He worked in the store on his vacations from school, and we were in awe of his being so smart that he was going to be a doctor. I suppose that none of us had ever met a medical student before. His parents were very proud of him, of course, but looking back I imagine that many of the long hours they worked were in large measure to pay for their son's education.

I can't even remember the young man's name, but I remember thinking even then that he would make a good doctor. He would be in his mid-sixties by now. I wonder where he is these days.

A man named Walt worked at the store, too, cleaning dishes and doing odd jobs. He lived upstairs from the store. He was thin, had wispy red hair, and his fingers were yellowed from all the Pall Malls he smoked one after another. Again in retrospect, he was probably a "poor soul" that the Fisher's had befriended and took care of. I do not recall him ever mentioning family of his own. Walt lived a hermit-like existence but seemed to enjoy the parade of kids who all got to know him.

My twin brother Jimmy also worked at the store for the last year or so before he was killed while in high school in an automobile accident just a few blocks away from Watchung Avenue. I can still see Jimmy in his apron, taking orders and getting a kick out of learning to make different kinds of sodas, to use the cash register and to make correct change. The Fishers liked him, and I was proud to have my brother working at the place where we all hung out.

I could not go into the store for weeks after Jimmy's death, because it was too painful for me.

The day I got up the courage to go back was a warm July day about two months after the accident. I just walked in and sat at the counter. I could feel the Fishers looking at each other and then at me, and then they both came over to where I was sitting. Mr. Fisher took the cigar out of his mouth, and Mrs. Fisher put her cloth down and nervously wiped her hands on her apron. "We were afraid you would never come back," she said, "but we would have understood." Mr. Fisher looked at his wife and nodded his head in agreement. "But we are glad you are back," she continued. "How are things going at home?"

I probably started to cry, although I didn't want to.

I told them what I could about so many things that had taken place in my family since and to some degree because of Jimmy's death. I said that we were all doing the best we could but that it was very difficult. I probably started to cry, although I didn't want to.

Mr. Fisher excused himself and went into the back of the store. I heard the rear door open and close.

Mrs. Fisher told me that people had been asking after my family: Walt, Mrs. Osgoode who also lived upstairs, the Greek couple next door who owned a small delicatessen, the Neumanns who ran the bakery a few stores away, and others who lived or worked on the block. They all constituted a real, extended family, and the Behrens, in our grief, had been adopted as part of that family. They mourned my family's loss, and we were all blessed because of their mourning.

I heard the back door open again, and Mr.

Fisher reappeared carrying on his arm a basket, covered with cellophane and done up with a ribbon, containing a bottle of red wine and some cheese. "For your family," he said as he awkwardly handed me the bundle, "with our condolences." He looked at me with tenderness and smiled, and then he looked around for his cigar.

I thanked them both and said that I had to get home. They asked me to come back often, and so I did. I returned to that little store throughout the years I was a seminarian and then a priest of the Archdiocese of Newark. Long after the Fishers were gone, and Walt and Mrs. Osgoode and the Greek couple and the Neumanns had either moved away or passed on, I still went back. And when I did I always remembered things old and yet ever new, things so needed wherever we human beings find ourselves—whether the streets of the old neighborhood, a newly yuppified block, a suburban housing development, the family farm, or a Trappist monastery outside of Atlanta.

We need the compassion expressed with wine and cheese, the simple gifts we give each other in times of sorrow. We need to become one extended family, where the pain of one is shared by all. We need to realize that such love is born only from suffering—which is perhaps the most profound and enduring mystery of all.

The Girl Who Tried to Taste the Moon

The pier extended quite far, and the surf of the Atlantic swayed below. The ocean was calm and, as far as one could see, it glistened and rippled.

The pier was at Seaside Heights, a popular resort area on the Jersey shore, and was called Amusement Pier because there were rides and attractions for most of its length. At the end of the pier was an area where people could stand and gaze at the beauty of the ocean and the enormous expanse of the sky. On a summer night, the pier was ablaze with a dazzling array of thousands of colored lights that rose and fell and swayed with the rides. The smells of popcorn, pizza, sausages, hot dogs and the ocean itself blended to make an aroma that was unique.

Peals of laughter and delight filled the air and mixed effortlessly with the ceaseless sounds of the rides as they carried young and old far into the night sky. One ride, a large globe covered with small square pieces of glass, had long swings attached to it. The globe slowly turned, and those who rode the swings glided peacefully out and over the surf. It was my favorite ride, and I would

31

sometimes stay on for an hour, riding in the sky high above the sea, my hands tightly holding the chains of the swing.

One evening, I walked to the end of the pier. The sky was filled with stars, and an enormous moon appeared to be rising out of the ocean. I still do not know why the moon, at particular places and times, appears to be much larger than usual. From where I stood on the pier that night, though, it looked many times its normal size. Its craters and valleys were easily discernible, and even the shadows of its mountains could be seen. It seemed so large and so near that it could be touched. Which is exactly what a small child was trying to do.

She was a little girl, seated in a stroller right near me. Her parents had come to the end of the pier, and the magic of the moon had worked its charm on them. They were kissing and holding hands as they contemplated the beauty of the moon.

They were kind of ignoring their daughter, but I observed that the little girl appeared fascinated by the rising moon, which was bathing the ocean with a generous amount of light that spread as it rose. She could not seem to take her eyes off of the enormous orb of yellow that was before her.

Suddenly, she reached out and tried to touch the moon. Then she laughed and squealed as she put her fingers to her mouth. I have no idea what she was trying to do, but it looked to me as if she were trying to take a piece of the delicious-looking moon and taste it.

Is it any wonder that we would want to taste the moon?

We live in an age when we too readily leave to science the answers to questions concerning the true nature of all things. If the ultimate meaning of life is inseparable from the deepest longings of our hearts, however, then perhaps poets and moon tasters of all ages are closer to the real answers than the Noble-laureates might be.

Perhaps there is a lesson for all of us to learn from that little girl on the boardwalk. Physicists tell us that everything that exists enjoys a relationship of reciprocity with everything else. The tiniest bits of matter are made for each other and somehow "know" each other, even though separated by millions of miles and, in some instances, by time itself. So we humans long for the rest of creation, for the near yet at once so far, for that which exists both in and out of time. We hunger for love that never dies and for eternal life for ourselves and those we know and love. We pray that our losses be redeemed, that there is in fact a greater power who hears our prayers and knows our needs.

Is it not true that when we want to describe the truth of what lies in our hearts, we take our images from the vastness of the sea, the heights of the mountains, the fire of the stars? Is it any wonder that we would want to taste the moon?

A Dying Woman's Gift

Every so often we have an experience that breaks through to the heart like a gush of wisdom, love, pain and strength all at once. It comes from no exact place but it illumines everything. Like an unexpected gust of wind, it cleans, reveals, sweeps away until everything seems holy.

I had such a wondrous experience one day several years ago, before I entered the monastery. It involved two meals, a moth, love and a dying woman.

It was the day before Halloween, and I had dinner that night with friends, Jean and Carl and their three boys. I sat in their home, listening to the flow of words that summarized the events of the day and touched on the more intimate concerns that bind all families together.

From where I sat, I could see a moth outside a large patio sliding door, beating its wings against the glass, drawn to the light hanging above the kitchen table. It was an out-of-season moth, destined by fate and instinct to beat its wings futilely and alone. Seemingly, it had no other reason for its existence other than to remind me that some things have no purpose.

Before dinner, grace was said, with all of us holding hands. Young Matthew had a headache and did not feel like eating, so he excused himself and headed up to his bedroom. His twin, Daniel, complained about having to get up so early every morning to catch the school bus. He then began to make an impression of the bus driver's face, twisting his cheeks and mouth beyond all normal proportion. He seemed satisfied that he had "captured" the right contortion so as to resemble the not-well-liked bus driver, so he let go of the face and laughed at himself.

After dinner, Jean brought out a Halloween cake, decorated with orange icing and candles. Matthew had by then returned to the table, his face a bit puffy. He and Daniel blew out the candles in a pro forma way, not making any wishes. Their older brother David soon came in, not hungry and annoyed that he had to work late and that there was to be a party at his workplace the next day to which he was expected to go in costume. His brothers made fun of him and continued eating the orange colored cake. David left in a huff to go work out at the YMCA.

The moth was still at the window, now being carefully watched by a slightly higher order of created being, Fluffy the cat, who sat before the glass watching the erratic meanderings of the lost and tantalizing insect. The cat's head moved back and forth in tandem with the movements of the moth.

Earlier that same day, I had eaten lunch with Chickie and Rose, who had been friends with each other for more than thirty years. Chickie had called me earlier in the week to tell me that Rose had terminal cancer. She was afraid that Rose would not live to see Christmas. As we sat together at Chickie's house, Rose talked about her job, her children, and her husband. She spoke carefully about those things that meant the most to her, showing me pictures of her new granddaughter. She ate well, which surprised Chickie, but after an hour she looked at the clock and said that she had to get going.

I walked her to her car, and as she was opening the car door I told her that I knew about her illness and would be glad to talk or just be with her if she needed me. She smiled, and said that she was not afraid of dying. She took my hand and gently squeezed it, telling me some of the many things that she wanted to do before she died. That afternoon, she said, she was going Christmas shopping.

I kissed Rose on the cheek and she drove off. I stood there and waved, but she did not look back.

Going into the house, I sat with Chickie for a while. She told me that when she found out about Rose's disease, all she could say to her friend was "I love you."

I finally left Chickie's house, and went to Jean and Carl's, with Rose very much on my mind. She was preparing to leave "here" and was probably remembering scenes from her life just like the one I was experiencing now—quiet moments with family, all vivid to her in a new and sharply painful way.

> *I will always have the image of her, driven to buy and wrap one more present for each of those she loved.*

I watched the cat and the moth. I saw an upset older son and heard the laughter of younger brothers. I listened to the day's worries. As the family rounded off the closing moments of another day of their lives together, I thought of Rose, gathering gifts as we ate, moving from aisle to aisle in a nearby mall, determined to leave behind gifts chosen and wrapped with love.

As I connected her with what was transpiring before me, it was if the room were spun from pure gold. The words of the family were sheer loveliness. The laughter of the boys echoed the grace of the entire universe. The kitchen light glowed like a jewel, and the cat and the moth seemed to be engaged in something of eternal significance.

The memory of that day and those two meals—so close together and somehow connected—has incredible power for me.

I do not know the gifts Rose bought for others that night, but this memory is mine: I will always have the image of her, driven to buy and wrap one more present for each of those she loved.

"I love you."

Those words do more than fill the air. They carry the very meaning of the life that is God's. They whisper once, three times, a million times, that nothing is in vain—not the beating of the wings of a moth against a pane of cold glass, nor the blowing out of candles on a bright orange cake, nor the careful selection of gifts by a dying woman.

The Presence of God

Father Pat was born and raised in Tanzania. I met him only once, quite a few years ago when he came to raise money for the missions at the parish where I was an associate pastor. I connected with him right away, because we both liked to talk about philosophy, religion and the separate worlds we inhabited.

As we sat in the rectory living room and spoke that evening, we could hear boys playing touch football in our church parking lot. They used to play there almost every summer night, and I used to sit on the front steps of the rectory and watch them. That night they had a special appeal to me in light of what Pat and I were discussing. We spoke of essences and ways of arriving at them, using the exotic language of philosophy. But what we were getting at was happiness and love and the existence of God, and it occurred to me that the kids already had all that figured out instinctively.

Pat had been raised in a village in Africa. His people did not have libraries, computers, televisions, and the like. Youngsters were taught by their elders what was deemed important, and they would all chant together until the presence of God was very real to them. Pat said that the children simply *knew* that God was present. Then he laughed and corrected himself. No, he said, it wasn't a *knowing* as much as it was a *feeling*.

> *Wouldn't it be a wondrous thing if we could experience everything as grace, believe that there is nothing that is not of God, accept every day as an invitation to leave the shelter of our minds and see, touch and rejoice in divine life?*

It struck me that night, and it continues to strike me as I remember it from behind the monastery walls, how differently Pat and his people experienced God from most of us in the West. Is it possible that because of our lingering insistence on tracking God with the radar of our minds that we refuse to venture a trusting yet uncertain journey toward God with our hearts, our feelings, our intuition? Wouldn't it be a wondrous thing if we could experience everything as grace, believe that there is nothing that is not of God, accept every day as an invitation to leave the shelter of our minds and see, touch and rejoice in divine life?

The boys playing football in a parking lot in Newark and the young people chanting with their elders in Tanzania already experienced the presence of God—whether they could articulate it or not. Religion should not concern itself with what is "in" or "out," what is "sacred" or not. It should not become a frame that holds us but rather a force that helps us burst through all frames. It should be inclusive, hopeful, not afraid of looking in the wrong places. True religiosity has a self-correctiveness to it that leaves plenty of room for art, poetry, dance, chanting and playing a game of ball on a hot summer's night.

Ours is an age and a society that seeks God more than ever. Our minds are understandably weary from the overload of thought that seems to have exhausted itself and does not know how to be refreshed. But God is present despite our effort or lack of effort, despite our awareness or lack of awareness.

The Face of Pain

His name I cannot remember, though his face is as vivid to me as it was when I last saw him almost fifteen years ago. He was nine years old and used to come to early Mass with his mother almost every morning at a parish in Newark where I was an associate pastor for many years. They sat in the first pew, and I soon realized that she was coaching him in the routines for being an altar server.

The day finally came for the meeting of new servers, and his mother dropped the boy off before any of the other kids arrived. She told me that he was eager to serve Mass but was worried that he might not get along with the others. I asked her why, and she said that he was a loner. I noticed later at the practices that he did keep his distance, but he proved to be trustworthy and polite. In fact, he had an eagerness to please that broke my heart, for I sensed that he was hurting very much in his young life.

I asked the pastor about the boy and he told me that there were serious marriage problems in the home. He did not elaborate, but I then understood the boy's sadness and need for acceptance.

Several weeks ago, while I was praying before the Blessed Sacrament, I thought about the boy again. His face simply "arrived" in my mind's eye, even though I could not think of anything that would have triggered it. Perhaps I was praying for all the people in pain in the world, and the boy's face simply embodies that suffering for me.

I thought back to those first months after I met him. He looked undernourished and sad even when he smiled. It was the kind of smile that pleads for help and recognition. He did fine as an altar boy, and then for some reason stopped coming. I never saw him again. The pastor said that the family had moved away, and I remember thinking that there must have been financial problems that forced them to relocate.

Ever since that time, that little boy's face has been to me a window or a mirror through which I observed something that exists in each of us. It is said that human pain is an invariant, that is, it is one of the few constants that all people of all cultures experience. To be human is, at least partially, to suffer pain. But pain is not only something that happens to us from the outside. At its most fundamental level, it is an ongoing part of the human condition and it comes from within. Yet we are constantly hit from all sides—in the media, in the taken-for-granted ethos of our times—with the idea that pain is abnormal, unusual, unacceptable. We are made to believe that when and where pain exists, it can simply be eradicated by taking the right medication, finding the right therapist or support group, thinking the right way, reading the right book, moving to the right place.

> *Ever since that time, that little boy's face has been to me a window or a mirror through which I observed something that exists in each of us.*

That little boy's face speaks volumes to me. In it I see the hurt in all of us, the hurt that comes from our estrangement from God and from each other. It is a hurt that is not going to go away, but it is one that we can make more tolerable for one another if we really try.

A "Grace Unknown"

Many years ago, I visited Lourdes, France, the site of the appearances by Our Lady to a young girl named Bernadette. I was then in my early twenties, but some scenes from the visit are still quite vivid in my mind's eye. I remember a rainy afternoon and a woman selling beautiful flowers from a cart. She was dressed in a plastic rain coat and sat beneath a large umbrella. I took a photograph of her, and was impressed later with how the streets glistened in the finished black and white print.

I recall the large crowds and being particularly impressed by the candlelight procession that was held each evening. A line of pilgrims stretched for what seemed miles, and their flickering candles could be seen far into the distance—a long, magic road of soft light that moved with majesty and reverence towards the shrine.

The shrine itself was simple: a statue of Mary, made of a pure white material, nestled in a grotto. Water ran nearby, believed to carry with it the favors and blessings of the Mother of God. Vigil lights burned in blue and red glass, lit in hope for miracles yet to come and in gratitude for those already granted. A sense of the miraculous permeated the air. On the walls of the grotto were hung many hundreds of canes, crutches, braces and other joyously discarded helps for those once disabled and now cured. At any given time during our visit there, the disabled and ill could be readily seen throughout the crowds.

I confess that back then I did not give much thought to the miraculous. If asked what I thought about it all, I probably would have responded that I wanted proof, to see and experience for myself—on my own terms—what seemingly defied rational explanation. Although I was not able to explain all the discarded crutches and the like, I was also aware that not all who made the trip to Lourdes were cured. Perhaps I wanted to believe but did not know how. Or, perhaps the circumstances of my life then did not warrant a need to believe. I was young, my life was good; my desperate and hurting straits were still far down the road. You might say that I was skeptical, but in fact I was quite self contained. Nothing outside of what I could provide from my own resources seemed necessary or even desirable. I was, in short, religiously smug.

On Sunday, my companions and I attended Mass in the large and beautiful shrine. The homily was by a priest who spoke French, and I knew enough French back then to follow what he was saying. He was an older man, and he spoke with gentleness. He said that he knew that many in the church had come to Lourdes with specific requests for a miracle, which he felt was well and good. But he went on to develop his thoughts about grace *"inconnu"* or "unknown." Although we may not receive what we specifically ask, he insisted, much more than what we request is indeed given, no one is ever deprived of grace, and grace arrives "unknown" in wondrously unexpected ways.

> ### *Perhaps I wanted to believe but did not know how.*

This old priest seemed to want desperately to share a sense that life is an unending shower of blessings. As I write this memory, I somehow associate his words with my father's death in a small hospital in Louisiana, not far from the monastery.

Dad had been ill for some time, and we knew that his life was nearing an end. He knew that, too. His wife and his sons and daughters, knowing in our hearts that he was suffering and would die, prayed for many miracles. The most obvious one—that Dad would get better, leave the hospital, return home again and resume his former life—seemed beyond hope. Yet we wanted something good and tangible to come from the terrible pain he was experiencing and from the sorrow of losing him from our lives. We prayed for grace, but it was a "grace unknown."

Dad did die, and it was a beautiful death. His family shed many tears of grief, but we did experience a small miracle in the many good and loving people—family, friends, doctors, nurses, ministers and others—who visited him and gave him whatever love and care they had to give. They formed a long, magic road of soft light that moved with majesty and reverence through his hospital room. They provided my father with all he really needed to die in peace.

They were "grace unknown"—words from a sermon I heard many years ago and only now understand.

God in the Details

When I was first entering the monastery, I shared with a friend of mine that I was afraid my friendships back home would be lost or at least frozen in time, that I would not know how to keep them alive and a vital part of me.

My friend smiled at me and said that all those I love would go with me and grow in my heart in new and deeper ways. "Just continue to love all of us," she said, "and God will take care of the details." I think I have learned what she meant from my friends Jimmy and Mary.

Jimmy and Mary own a farm in northern New Jersey. I served in a parish there for several years shortly after I was ordained. That was over twenty-five years ago, and I have gone to their home for dinner often over the years. Jimmy is a big man with a ready smile who cannot do enough for you. Mary is sweet and bright and giving. After dinner, we would go to their living room and sit and talk for hours. The room was large and comfortable, with all sorts of unique things from their travels and antique shows. There was a large tropical fish tank in the corner, which bubbled away as we chatted. Through a large window that faced the back yard I could see the trees and the fences where they kept exotic animals they raised for zoos: horses, ostriches, emus, goats, miniature deer. On many a warm summer night, Jimmy would walk me around the farm and show me the newer additions. He was always proud of the animals and delighted in showing them off to me.

When I first started to write, I would type up my essays (this was before the advent of word processing and e-mail) and bring them with me when I went to their home. They would put them aside, and by the next time I visited they would have read them and told me how they liked them. One night, Jimmy seemed especially animated when we sat down after dinner. "I have to tell you something," he said. "The piece you wrote about Pine Street is the best ever."

I had given them an essay the week before about one of the streets in the town near them. "It's the details," Jimmy proclaimed. "I could picture everything: the Chinese restaurant with the little Buddha statue and candle; the kids playing in the street; the liquor store on the corner; the lady on the porch across the street. Know what? Mary and I just had to look at the street again. We actually drove into town, and it's all there, just like you said."

Jimmy was right. I did embellish that essay with a lot of details, and I could remember hesitating to do so while I was writing it. I wanted to make a point, I remember, and did not want to have the details get in the way. Yet here was Jimmy, enthralled more with the details than with whatever point I was trying to make, enthusiastic enough to hop in a van and drive twelve miles to check them out, as he said, "for real."

> ***"Just continue to love all of us,"***
> ***she said, "and God will take care of***
> ***the details."***

Jimmy writes to me frequently. His penmanship is beautiful and he always uses fine onionskin paper. I love his letters and have told him so.

They are filled with details—about his wife, his sons and grandchildren, his exotic animals. I can experience them right on the page, almost as if I were still walking around the farm.

But I am here in my room, and it is getting late. The monastic day starts early, so I will go to bed soon.

I will write Jimmy and Mary tomorrow morning, long before the sun rises over both Georgia and New Jersey. I know now that our friendship will last our lifetimes and will develop and grow...as long as we all pay attention to the details.

The Parade

I like the sense of proportion and perspective that thrives in the small town of Madisonville, Louisiana, near where my parents moved after they retired. The conversations that go on in the barber shop or beauty parlor bring global things down to manageable proportions. The old library is roughly the size of the average drive-in bank but is well used—even more so than the new large library that is some distance from the town.

One of my visits home from the monastery coincided with Mardi Gras. My parents asked me if I wanted to go with them that afternoon to the parade. I declined at first, thinking that they wanted to drive to New Orleans for one of the grand-scale parades there. But Mom said that the parade was right in Madisonville, so we all went over to see it.

It was indeed to be a small parade, on a small street in a small town, with low tech and few expectations. The floats were lined up at the end of the tree-lined main avenue, waiting to begin their slow, brief journey into the spotlight.

People watched from the porches of homes, welcoming friends and strangers alike to stop for something to drink and eat. Finally, the signal was given and the parade began. There were quite a few people lining the street, sitting on lawn chairs and clapping and cheering as the floats approached. It seemed that every organization in town was represented on one float or another, and I noticed that there was a great degree of reciprocal recognition shared between those on the floats and those on the streets. Everybody, in short, knew and liked one other, at least for that afternoon, and a genuine sense of neighborliness filled the March air.

> *In our younger seasons, we raise our hearts and hands, hoping to catch whatever love may come our way.*

The king and queen of the parade sat on the most brightly colored float, tossing shiny coins into the air in the direction of people who approached as the float glided by. The setting sun was a perfect backdrop to this small and colorful drama that unfolded on each block.

When they reached us, my mother raised her hands and caught three coins. Children scrambled around her, laughing and snatching coins from the air and off the street. Some of the children, however, were too small or too slow and were not able to catch any of the coins. Mom noticed their plight and, with great maternal pleasure, gave her coins to the disappointed children nearest her.

I watched the float pass into the golden sun and thought of the great parade of life. In our younger seasons, we raise our hearts and hands, hoping to catch whatever love may come our way. But with age and wisdom—and after more than a few parades—we learn to find delight in giving our love away, becoming all the richer for it.

Therefore I intend to keep on reminding you of these things, though you know them already and are established in the truth that has come to you.

2 Peter 1:13

Brother Life,
Sister Death

About twenty years ago, I used to bring the Eucharist to a woman named Katrina. She was in her late fifties and was dying at home from lung cancer. I remember her room as if I had been there yesterday. She collected antique lamps, and they warmed the room with a soft yellow light. I still think of her every time I see a Tiffany lamp or a kerosene lantern.

But it was Katrina who was the true light in that room.

She was not in a lot of pain, but she knew that she was dying. The smell of death was in the room. Whatever antiseptics were used could not fully conceal the smell of her disease. She was embarrassed by it and used to cover her mouth as she spoke to me, but I did not mind the odor.

She had remarkable faith and said things to me that I did not understand then. She had gone through whatever treatments were available and was weary and further weakened from them. She was not "resigned" to her approaching death, yet she was not bitter either. She welcomed death as a benevolent stranger—an unknown person she wanted to befriend, even though she knew that person would take her life.

I found something of God in Katrina. God spoke to me through her suffering, her loving, her hoping and her dying.

One morning, she asked me to hold her hand and pray with her. She gently clasped my hand and squeezed it just a bit, closing her eyes and smiling. We prayed, or rather *she* prayed. (I did not know what prayer really was back then.) She whispered prayers of love and hope for her children and her husband, and prayed to make the most of what little time she had left.

Then she looked down at her wasted body and addressed the cancer that had darkened and eaten away her lungs. "Strange friend," she said, "my disease that eats so close to my heart, I am at peace with you. *You* will bring me to God."

She comforted herself with her uncanny faith and confidence, transforming her disease from an enemy to a friend. She whispered softly to it and embraced its untimeliness.

Katrina certainly would not have been hostile to a cure. She loved life and would have welcomed more of it. She cried many times at the thought of not being able to touch, speak or simply be with her family. But she trusted God completely and allowed her weakness to become her strength.

"The secret is learning to love both, Father," she told me.

Looking back, I marvel at what a gift Katrina was to me, a young priest just beginning to grasp the implications of our faith. I was there with her family, holding her hand when she died, and I knew in the depths of my being that at the moment of death she did not cease to exist but became something more.

"Brother life, sister death," she used to call them. "The secret is learning to love both, Father," she told me.

Memories of Grace

A friend of mine stopped by the monastery recently, relating an experience that jolted him from his workaday routine. He was trying to fix a bug in his computer and was exasperated. Sitting back in his chair, he fixed his eyes on the whirling ceiling fan directly above him. Its blades turned slowly in a wide circling motion, and my friend was captivated by them for several moments. He said he had a sense of profound peace while watching the fan and felt the experience prompting him to remember a specific image or truth that he knew but had forgotten. It was, he said, as if God was trying to tell him something. The turning blades triggered an association he could not quite grasp or bring sharply into focus, but he knew that it was important.

The meaning of the experience became more and more elusive the more he tried to seize it through the manipulations of his conscious mind. Yet days later he remained fascinated by the intrusion of the lazily turning blades into his consciousness.

I have had similar experiences, and I also do not know what they mean. One is a time when I was a parish priest in Newark. It was six in the morning on a cold winter day. There was no visible rising of the sun because it was snowing heavily. I saw an old woman, all bundled up, shuffling heavily through the as yet unplowed church parking lot on her way to early Mass. As she passed beneath a streetlight, I saw thousands of snow flakes swirl and spin madly around her before coming to rest on the ground. Suddenly, she stopped before a statue of the Blessed Mother, bowed her head, placed her hand to her lips and then touched the base of the statue. After a moment, she walked on—out of the light and toward the church door.

> *These vague memories are somehow a window to our souls.*

And that's it! I don't know who the woman was, I don't know what the memory means, I don't know why it has such a hold on me. But there it is—just like my friend's twirling fan—going round and round in my mind, evoking an insight that remains just out of reach, pointing to some deep truth that I know but cannot articulate.

Here's another memory. I was ten or eleven years old and sitting in church one Sunday. I had a runny nose and kept sniffling. I was too old, I must have thought then, to wipe my nose on my sleeve yet too young to leave the pew and go looking for a tissue on my own. A lady with red hair tapped me on the shoulder from the pew behind me and handed me a wad of fresh tissues. I remember clearly, even to this day, how relieved I was.

There are no other memories from the hundreds of Masses I attended as a youth that stand out as sharply as this one does. I cannot call to mind, for example, an image of one priest saying Mass, but I remember that lady and can still see her face in my mind's eye. I think that I would recognize her immediately were I to see her again after all these years.

These vague memories are somehow a window to our souls. They disclose things to us, even prior to our consciousness or interpretation of them. Bidden or not bidden, the image of the old woman, walking against the cold wind, determined to go to Mass on a dark, harsh winter morning, comes to me. My friend, mesmerized by a fan, watches the blades turn and turn, feeling his heart move toward something he knows but cannot quite put his finger on. I remember a red-haired lady's single act of kindness to me and yet cannot recall anything else of that day or so many other days. It is as if some memories have a life and intent of their own. They seem to have their own reasons for coming, for staying, for leaving, even for hiding their meaning from our hearts and minds.

Yet how beautiful that old woman, gently kissing the Madonna in the swirling snow.

How vibrant the lady's red hair as she handed me the salvific tissue.

How hypnotic that ceiling fan.

Might they all be calling us to a deeper reality, a divine presence? Might they be memories of grace?

A Circus of Surprises

When I lived near New York City, I used to go to Washington Square, a small park in the heart of Greenwich Village. On a summer's day, if I was lucky enough to find a place to sit on one of the park's benches, I would stay for hours, people watching. It was a circus of surprises.

There was a man who walked around on stilts, with makeup on his face and a Mohawk haircut.

Numerous jugglers threw their colored balls and pins into the air before delighted crowds of people.

Old men sat at tables playing chess, checkers and other games. Some of them had their dogs with them, who seemed to enjoy the human spectacle parading before their eyes as much as I did.

Vendors galore sold their goods on the fringes of the park. Soda, popcorn, hot dogs and chestnuts were the usual fare. Just outside the park, others had watches, jewelry, incense and books for sale, spread out on rugs on the sidewalk.

There were fortune tellers who plied their talent from tables placed underneath the trees.

The area had a real carnival atmosphere to it.

I remember one man who had set up a little podium and was warning his listeners about the imminent coming of the last days. Well versed in the symbolism of the Apocalypse, he hammered at his small audience with ways and means of saving their souls before the fiery end. I was pleased to note that the man placed a box in front of the podium, hoping for donations. He must not have thought that the end was all that near!

I marveled at a man on a unicycle who seemed to find exquisite delight in weaving his way through the crowded sidewalks. He was young, had earrings, and sported colorful running shorts and a tie-dyed, tight-fitting shirt.

There were musicians who played flutes, guitars, violins, drums and countless other instruments, their empty music cases opened at their feet, hoping that onlookers would toss in a few coins.

Artists created picturesque scenes right on the sidewalks of the park, using chalks and pastels. It amazed me that they would put so much effort into their work, knowing that its beauty would be washed away with the next rain or dirtied by the feet of those who would soon walk over it.

> *It seems to me that the Church of all places should be a circus of surprises—not necessarily the kind I found in Washington Square but rather the kind that encourages us to take risks, to resist the predictable and the taken-for-granted, to lovingly support one another when we take roads that turn out to be dead ends.*

There were few restraints on human expression in the park. Lovers kissed and caressed freely—women kissing men, men kissing women, men kissing men, women kissing women. Young children of all colors and nationalities played together. The square was a kaleidoscope of tastes and cultures. Each slight turn of my head offered another fascinating scene. I used to wonder what I was missing elsewhere in the park if I kept my attention riveted too long in one place.

I suppose that I looked very conventional, sitting there on my bench. I actually envied those who dared to dress or act wildly, who would spend hours creating beauty for free, knowing that it would soon vanish.

Now that I look back from my current venue behind cloistered walls, what appealed most to me about Washington Square was the element of surprise. It seems to me that the Church of all places should be a circus of surprises—not necessarily the kind I found in Washington Square but rather the kind that encourages us to take risks, to resist the predictable and the taken-for-granted, to lovingly support one another when we take roads that turn out to be dead ends.

After all, we are the followers of the biggest surprise of all: the God who actually became a human being and was born—surprise of surprises—of what was the ultimate in lowly, obscure and unlikely origins. We believe that by this act God has turned all of creation into one, big, slowly unwrapping gift box, bearing within it things "eyes have not seen and ears have not heard."

We Christians should act as if life were one big Washington Square. That is the good news the Church has to offer.

The Rose

A long time ago, when I was a young parish priest, I raised roses. One day, a woman friend of mine asked if she could have a particular rose that stood out in the garden from all the rest. So I went into the rectory and found a scissors and carefully cut a beautiful salmon colored rose from the bush, taking care to cut a long stem. I gave the rose to my friend and she placed it next to her cheek to feel the softness of its petals. She smelled it and smiled at its fragrant loveliness.

It was, I thought to myself, a near perfect rose. Yet there were others—faded whites and reds and creams—that were wilted and sagging, dying beyond their usefulness. We both ignored them, but I remember wondering later if anyone had stood before them and admired their beauty before it had been lost.

My friend took the rose home and placed it in the best vase she owned, a Waterford. She placed a penny and an aspirin in the water to keep the rose fresh, for they supposedly would do something to the water to stall, for a while, the decay of the rose. I remember stopping by her house a few days later, and the rose indeed still looked fresh and beautiful.

Not long ago, I left the monastery for a day and went to a nearby shopping mall with another monk. The mall was crowded, and we walked down the large, wide aisles, gazing at the shoppers and looking into the store windows. The stores were filled with things comedian Billy Crystal might describe as "marvelous." There were jewels and furs and leathers, designer clothes and costly fragrances, sporting goods, silverware, gold and platinum rings, all laid out in one window after another beneath soft and alluring lights. Music played as we walked, softly accenting the atmosphere as we moved from one shop window to the next. We were hungry and stopped at the large food court for something to eat. Even there, fullness abounded. There were many cultural delicacies in a variety of different booths.

> *Many mystics have long testified to the existence of a higher state of consciousness—an experience of being one with all that is.*

After lunch, I sat in the mall and grew quiet, for amidst all that abundance there was nothing I really wished to buy (even if I had any money, which I didn't!) For some reason, I recalled the salmon colored rose. The mall seemed like a garden filled with people of a variety of aspirations, accomplishments and failures. I found that my eyes and thoughts were attracted to some and not to others. Like my friend with the rose, I deemed some more worthy of being noticed than others.

Many mystics have long testified to the existence of a higher state of consciousness—an experience of being one with all that is. But most of us usually see this dimly at best.

As one rose is eyed for its beauty, the others fade from site. Likewise, as we differentiate among people, we lose sight of what is good and common among all people.

From now on, I'm not going to cut any roses. They are all part of the same bush, the same beauty, the same existence.

Walker Percy and the American Express Card

People often ask me why I started writing at a relatively late age. (I was in my forties when I first started sending out articles for publication.) I have one person to thank, and this little memory of grace is about him.

The Kumquat was a bookstore in Covington, Louisiana. I frequented it every time I visited my parents after they retired there many years ago. It was owned by author Walker Percy's daughter, and I always went there on Tuesdays, when Walker's wife, Bunt Percy, was working. She would gladly show me the well-stacked shelves and in particular the collection of her late husband's novels and essays, displayed prominently to the left just inside the front door. Bunt has a weakness for good conversation and good soup, and there was an eatery right next door to the bookstore. So we had many happy meals together.

Over ten years ago, when I was still a parish priest in Newark and trying to decide what to do with the rest of my life, I was in graduate school, trying to come up with a dissertation topic for a Ph.D. in religion and society. I had reached the point beyond exasperation and despair; there is no name for the frustration I was experiencing.

I was staying with my parents in Covington and knew that Walker Percy, the acclaimed southern novelist, lived just a few miles away. I had already read several dissertations on his writings and found them intriguing. Perhaps, I thought, I could add something to the body of knowledge about this great Catholic American author.

I had heard about the Kumquat and went in one day and bought plenty of books by and about Walker Percy. The bill came to well over $150.00, and I was glad that I had my American Express card. I purchased the books with the card, and when the lady at the cash register asked for my telephone number I gave my parents' number.

I remember going home with my books in a yellow plastic bag and refusing to tell my dad how much they cost. I mumbled something to him about their being very modestly priced, but little did I know what a bargain they were.

That afternoon, I sat and read through some of the essays in *Lost in the Cosmos*, a collection of satirical essays by Walker Percy. My mom called me out of my reverie when it was time for dinner, and during the course of the meal I told my parents how excited I was about Percy's writings. I thought that I could soon come up with a workable topic on him for my dissertation.

> *What I received from him was what I truly needed, and that's why I call it "grace."*

Shortly after dinner, the telephone rang and Mom answered it.

When my mother gets excited, she blushes and her voice rises a little bit above its norm. I could tell that the telephone call was something out of the ordinary.

It was Walker Percy himself on the line. He wanted to speak to "the man who had bought so many books."

I will never forget how nervous I was when Mom handed me the receiver. I took the phone and introduced myself. I told him that I was a priest, loved his writings and was desperately in need of a dissertation topic.

He invited me to his home for lunch the next day.

I lay awake long into the night with anticipation. In the morning I actually went and got a haircut. Since I did not bring any good shoes on my visit, Dad let me borrow his. I also wore one of his best shirts.

I carefully followed the directions that the writer had given me, particularly keeping in mind his warning to watch out for their big Doberman. Walker Percy greeted me as I pulled in front of the house, and we went inside. He introduced me to his dog, and together we put the pooch at ease.

Walker (he insisted that I call him that) and I sat in the back room of their house, a large sun-filled room with a window overlooking the Boguefalaya River, and chatted over drinks and lunch for several hours. We spoke of the Church, the priesthood, American and Southern culture and, especially, about writing.

I told Walker that I had always wanted to write but that something held me back. That was early in the conversation, but as he walked me to my car several hours later he must have re-membered what I said, because he told me that I should write what I feel and—more impor-tantly—that I should always write with hope. He said that because I am a Christian and a Catholic priest I am "stuck with a wondrous message" and had little choice but to write about it.

This was to be the first of several times that

we met over the next few years.

We also exchanged letters that are among the few possessions I kept after I entered the monastery. I remember when I had my very first article published in 1989. It was in the *National Catholic Reporter,* which has since published many of my essays, and was about the holiness and hope I observed in a group of people who worked at Andy's Diner in Newark. Walker wrote back a warm letter of congratulations. (It is interesting that an editor from ACTA Publications also saw that article and included it in a book of readings on the spirituality of work. Over ten years later, that same editor published my first book, *Grace Is Everywhere.* So a large part of my writing career can be traced back to the encouragement of Walker Percy.)

In late 1990, Walker's letters stopped. My mom told me that she had heard that he was quite ill and that it did not look good. He died in the spring of 1991.

I wrote to his wife, Bunt, and later attended a memorial service for him that was held at Saint Ignatius Church in Manhattan. I sat in the back of the packed church and did not get a chance to speak with Bunt that day, but when I went to visit my parents shortly after Christmas that year I called her to express my condolences. She asked me to come over to the house for lunch, and we watched a football game together and chatted about a lot of things, including how much her husband had influenced my life.

She told me that she wanted to show me something, and taking me by the hand she took me into Walker's study.

> *He said that because I am a Christian and a Catholic priest I am "stuck with a wondrous message" and had little choice but to write about it.*

She said that the room was just as he had left it when he died. She smiled and pointed to what looked like a music stand near Walker's desk. There on the stand was an article that I had sent him about my brother's death. I was stunned to see it and yet very proud. He had written a few notes in the margins, but I did not want to disturb anything, so I did not pick up the paper to read what he had written. To this day I do not know what he said, but it is not important. What is important is that such a great man would spend even a few moments reading and commenting on something a fledgling author wrote.

I gave up my American Express card when I entered the monastery, but I am glad that I once used it to buy some books. I never did come up with a dissertation topic, never did get that doctoral degree. But Walker Percy encouraged me to write with hope about what I feel, and that is what I have always tried to do. What I received from him was what I truly needed, and that's why I call it "grace."

The Stained-Glass Slippers

It is an image that comes from a magazine I read many years ago. What first caught my eye was the picture that accompanied the article. It was a photograph of ballerina slippers—old, worn, frayed at the toes. The once shiny satin was torn and dirty.

The story was written by the woman who had kept the slippers from her childhood, holding on to them for these many years. It seems that as a little girl her heart's desire had been to dance. In the magazine, she recalled imagining herself on a great stage, dancing ballet. In those dreams, she saw herself dancing beautifully and gracefully, seemingly without effort. She envisioned the woman she so desired to become— dancing as if floating on air, affording magical delight to thousands.

When the little girl was old enough, her mother had bought her first slippers, the ones in the photograph. Then began years of hard practice. As the woman of her imagination danced and swirled in her dreams, the real little girl of flesh and blood stumbled and fell. She ached with sore feet, torn ligaments and many bruises, all accompanied by prolonged periods of disappointment and heartache as progress was slow and unrewarding. Still the little girl picked herself up time after time with her mother's support and encouragement. There would be many more sets of slippers, but the first she kept.

> ### *She and the lovely woman of her dreams became one and the same.*

As the years passed, the falls became far less frequent. The young woman mastered the art of movement and began to dance with grace and power. She and the lovely woman of her dreams became one and the same. Now grown to adulthood, the woman keeps the old slippers as a reminder that what is truly loved and dreamed for is indeed possible—but only with effort, determination and loving support.

I look at the beautiful church at our monastery and think of the countless, long-forgotten people who gave from what little they had that there might be stained-glass windows, marble altars, and many things of loveliness and beauty here.

What is not reflected in the bricks and mortar, however, are their dreams—dreams that were realized through sacrifice and hard work. These are the sacrifices that make the church real and breathing and reflective of God.

I would like to raise one more stained-glass window high in our church. In the center of that window would be a pair of worn-out ballerina slippers.

Joe

Early Christmas Eve many years back, I was looking out the front window of the rectory and noticed a man sprawled across the front steps of the church.

I recognized Joe, a young man suffering from alcoholism. His disease was far advanced, and I am quite sure that his strong constitution was the only thing that had staved off an early death.

Joe was in his early thirties. He was homeless and had gone through detox at a nearby hospital several times. He stopped by the rectory frequently for food, a cigarette, a cup of coffee or a few dollars. He slept anywhere he could find shelter, which was usually beneath a nearby railroad trestle or in a large heated doorway in the front of a shopping mall several blocks away from the church.

The memory of him lying there that night sticks in my mind. His isolation and despair was in such contrast to the full and expectant gatherings that would soon be taking place that night in homes and places of worship all over the world. It seemed that everyone that night, except Joe, was involved in the redemptive process.

I knew from experience that there was nothing at all we could do for Joe. Hank, our deacon, brought him inside and gave him some hot chocolate and a sandwich. We encouraged him to go to a nearby Salvation Army shelter, but Joe shook his head and headed back out into the night.

I thought about how God lived in Joe, how God suffered in him, how God felt the cold concrete on his face and the sting of cold urine on his legs. The helplessness and hopelessness of any human life cannot be estranged from the reality of the God who loves every one of us, no matter what our situation or state in life. In the ever-so-human condition of Joe, God lived and waited as well, curled beneath a railroad trestle, within hearing distance of Yuletide carols and alleluias.

We Christians believe redemption—that blessed recovery of all things holy—to be an ongoing and mysterious process. We know that we shall all be redeemed in God's time and through God's love. It is something we all await. Joe will be saved, as will all who have been hurt or broken and seemingly put out of the human family.

I once tried to understand salvation as a singular, somehow approachable event—something that could be described with words between the covers of a fine textbook. I have come to accept it as being many seeds of living potential strewn throughout the universe, born and matured by the winds of mystery and providence. These seeds blossom only through the struggles of existence, in which the cross of Christ stands as the promise of eternal life.

> *The helplessness and hopelessness of any human life cannot be estranged from the reality of the God who loves every one of us, no matter what our situation or state in life.*

This is our only hope. It is a hope that prompts a recognition of the Joe that is within us all—a helplessness in need of a cup of coffee, a place of warmth and understanding, and the healing love of God.

Watching Hank feed Joe that night, I thought of the God who feeds all of us and yet still needs to be dried and fed and clothed and sheltered.

The Lady on the Bus

The #66 DeCamp is the bus I used to take from the Port Authority Bus Terminal in Manhattan back home to Montclair, New Jersey, when I was a parish priest there. I would go to Manhattan to see my brother John and then walk from his office on West 57th Street to the terminal on West 41st Street.

One night several years ago, I took the late bus and found a seat right in the front. I was glad because I liked looking out the large front window, watching the road glide smoothly beneath the bus.

A woman sat on my right. She had the window seat. She was young and pretty and could have been many things—a business executive, a secretary, a sales clerk. There was no way to know. She was nicely dressed and, like so many women who commute back and forth to Manhattan, she wore sneakers and kept her good shoes in a bag or left them at her workplace.

The bus pulled out into the night and wound its way down a long ramp and on through the Lincoln Tunnel. There was not much traffic at that time of night, and the bus moved easily along its route. I stared straight ahead, watching all that was before me, gazing at very familiar lights and buildings along Route 3. I was absorbed in whatever was on my mind for those few miles.

> *In a culture that easily reduces love to something akin to a possession, a right, a path of self-fulfillment that approaches self-gratification, it is hard to take seriously the kind of love that calls one out of oneself for the sake of others.*

Suddenly I felt a light something on my shoulder. The woman had dozed off and her head had come to rest on me. I felt a flush of panic lest she wake up and think me "forward" or worse. But I relaxed as best I could because I liked her being there and, frankly, it had been a long time since any woman had been that close to me—in a sleepily warm way, at least.

The bus rolled along the New Jersey highway. The intimate nearness of the woman made me think. I could smell the sweet fragrance of her hair. I wondered what she did for a living that made her so tired. Or maybe she had just let go of the cares of the day.

And so it was that we rode for miles. I began to wonder what it would be like, sharing my life with a woman. There was nothing at all "religious" about what I was thinking, at least in a formal sense, but I experienced for those few miles the sense of a shared comfort and vulnerability that can exist between two people—a sacred and inviolable space, where it is easy and natural to trust someone enough to fall asleep on his or her shoulder.

The bus took the sharp turn off Route 3 and wound its way onto Grove Street. The swaying of the bus wakened her. She looked up at me and said "Sorry" and smiled. I said it was okay and smiled back at her. We rode on in silence to Montclair. She soon reached up and pressed the stop button a few stops before mine. She gathered her things from the bin above, and I leaned back as she left her seat and climbed off the bus. I watched her as the bus pulled away and she departed to wherever she lived—perhaps to her husband and children.

As I sit and write these words, the memory of her makes me smile to myself in this quiet, celibate monastery. We speak of love here a lot, and much of our conversation has to do with learning love's ways as God would have us know them. In a culture that easily reduces love to something akin to a possession, a right, a path of self-fulfillment that approaches self-gratification, it is hard to take seriously the kind of love that calls one out of oneself for the sake of others. But that is exactly what the monastic vocation is about—just as it is the basis for every good marriage and family.

What warms me about the memory of that bus ride was seeing the woman find a "place" of peace and trust on my shoulder, a place where thought and worry stopped, where the ride was smooth and she could let go of her busy day and sleep in peace.

The Cleaning Ladies

There was a time I worked on Wall Street in New York, and I should not make a big deal out of it because it was not a very long period in my life. But it was a very rich one, even though I did not make a lot of money. I saw a lot, absorbed a lot, wondered a lot.

One night I worked late and was tired. It was a very cold night, and I walked from Pine and Water Streets across the tip of Manhattan to a park near the World Trade Center. I bought a cup of coffee, found an empty iron bench and sat down. Around me were works of art: life-sized statues of commuters—both men and women—looking very real in the shadows of night. These statues were already familiar to me. There is even one of a man just like me sitting on a bench just like mine. It was as if I had become frozen there in time.

I sipped the hot coffee and looked about. The Trade Center towers rose magnificently above me, some of their lights still on. In the distance the Hudson River flowed into New York harbor, and the lights of many large ships twinkled. I could see New Jersey's lights, too. All around me the shops were closed. Only the restaurants and bars were still open. The rush hour was long over and there were few people passing by.

Suddenly, large crowds of people filled the square. Mostly women, they came to clean the offices in the buildings. I'd guess there are tens of thousands of them in Manhattan any given night. The ones I saw that night came out of the subways, where they had arrived from the Bronx, Brooklyn, Queens, New Jersey and other parts of the metropolitan area. They carried bags and parcels and traveled in pairs, moving quickly through the city streets, anxious to get to the warmth of their workplaces and out of the bitter cold.

> *That is the way it has always been; that is the way it always will be.*

These women were struggling to make a better life for themselves and their families, and money was needed for that. I feel intrusive even now wondering about their lives, but I was captivated by them and believe they have something to teach all of us about the meaning of life and love and work and wealth.

I am now in a Trappist cloister in Georgia, and tonight in Manhattan I am sure the cleaning women are just arriving. They walk beneath towering signs of power and wealth and among frozen statues of business men and women. They may look around them in awe, but they have work to do, lives to live, children to feed, things to attend to. That is the way it has always been; that is the way it always will be.

I close my eyes and pretend I am in that park again, sitting unnoticed among the statues. I see the cleaning women pouring out of the subways—hundreds, even thousands of them. It is warm this evening, so maybe they would be walking slowly and laughing as they move toward their places of work. They are truth for me. I want to absorb all that I can learn from them—their values and their commitment and their motivation. And whatever I do in my life, I want desperately to give back to people like them something good.

Delivering the News

I took over Ernie's newspaper route when I was a teenager. He was going off to college, and I rode next to him on my bike for the last few days before he left. Ernie used to take one paper at a time, fold it as he rode and then toss it through the air onto the path or stoop leading to the customer's front door. I noticed that he hardly paused as the papers landed perfectly in the same spot every day, and he never looked back.

His bike had a large metal basket on the handlebars into which he placed a large canvas bag. The bag was white—though many deliveries had faded it to gray—with the lettering *"Newark Evening News"* in black gothic type on the front. The bag could hold fifty papers on an average day, though I remember that Fridays had especially fat editions and those days were a rough ride. I used to ponder the revelation that the more news there was, the more difficult my life became. (That little shard of wisdom has proved to contain much truth in my life.)

Ernie had a change machine, one of those silvery metal change makers that he wore on a belt. The ice cream man used to have the same kind of thing, and such a gadget was long an envy of mine. Without looking, Ernie could count out the exact amount of change and quickly be on his way. On his last day he took me collecting with him and told his customers that he would not be delivering the paper anymore and that—by the way—here was Jeff, who would be taking over the route. I remember people telling him to wait just a minute as they went back into the house and got five or ten dollars for him—a fortune in those days. The customers barely looked at me. I knew I would have to earn my place in their hearts…and pocketbooks.

It has been forty years now since I delivered those papers. The *Newark Evening News* stopped its presses long ago. And I would guess that there are not as many newspaperboys or newspapergirls today as there were back then.

I delivered papers in the 1960s, a time when so much of the news was heartbreaking. It was a time of war and social upheaval, riots and assassinations. But I was a kid whose interests back then did not move much beyond a new group called the Beatles.

One piece of news was delivered to me, however, that I absorbed with the unthinking receptivity of a child. It was the news that there were people like Ernie in the world—people who work hard, are skilled, efficient and dependable, and are kind to others. This is the good news I was given back then, and the memory of it warms me to this day.

> *I used to ponder the revelation that the more news there was, the more difficult my life became.*

I wonder where Ernie is today. He would be a few years older than I am, and I hope life has been kind to him. I'll bet he is still riding without looking back. So much grace has flowed into me from people like Ernie, who never made the news but delivered far more important news than he ever realized.

*"Do you have eyes, and fail to see?
Do you have ears, and fail to hear?
And do you not remember?"*

Mark 8:18

The Nickel Vase

Once, way before I entered the monastery, I went to a writer's conference in Boston. Even then, I guess, I knew that I wanted to communicate with others through the written word rather than by preaching and speaking.

The conference included classes in which the instructor read short stories written by the students. After each story was read, we students would critique it—usually not too insightfully and never very kindly.

One of the participants was a middle-aged woman who sat near me as her story was read. She squirmed and doodled on a pad as her words were absorbed by the class. When the teacher finished the story, the comments began. At first, we were gentle: "The characters are real," "there is a good flow," "the imagery is nice." The woman beamed as if she had finally discovered a group of people who recognized her talent and perceived her inner spirit.

In her story, however, was a five word sentence that read: "The vase cost a nickel." A man raised his hand and harrumphed, "No vase costs only a nickel." The dam was broken, and hands

shot up all over the room. There was an outpour-
ing of comments and opinions about the vase—
its cost, where it might have been purchased,
how it could have been so cheap. The author said
nothing but sat doodling with a fury.

Someone said that the price of a nickel threw
the rest of the story into a false light. Another
claimed to have seen a vase at a flea market in
Vermont priced at a mere three cents. Mean-
while, the writer kept making tighter and tighter
circles on her notepad.

Finally, she could take it no longer. She
stopped her doodling and stood up. Everyone
fell silent and stared at her. Her voice cracking
with emotion, she swore that the vase had cost
her a nickel and that she would never change
that detail, even if no one believed her story. Then
she started to cry, gathered her things and
stormed out of the room. We never saw her
again.

One student commented, "She really got
bent out of shape over a measly five cents."

But as I remember the event from behind
the cloister walls, I realize that the nickel was
never the issue. There were obviously other
things going on in the woman's life that our de-
bate triggered. We were all focused on this one
detail, and by the time she lost her composure

the beauty of her story no longer seemed to matter to anyone but her.

There are a lot of lessons in this little incident. Certainly her fellow students should have been more sensitive and perhaps she should have been less thin-skinned. Maybe the details in an article or story have to be believable, even if we have to manipulate the facts a little to make them so.

> *There are a lot of "nickel vases" in each of our lives that are important to us alone in ways that no one else can ever understand.*

But the main thing I took from the incident is the realization that we all cling to apparently insignificant things. When these are threatened or even questioned, it can cause us much pain. There are a lot of "nickel vases" in each of our lives that are important to us alone in ways that no one else can ever understand. Maybe we do not even understand them ourselves. But these vases are easily broken if not handled with care. They are possessions that—taken as a whole— form our personal identity and put us in touch with the inherent goodness we humans share.

So, if someone says that a vase cost a nickel, perhaps we should take that statement at "vase value." (Sorry about the pun, but I couldn't resist.) It may have been worth only small change, but that woman's memory of her vase may have formed the basis for her real wealth.

Little Stuart

When I was a kid, my family lived on a dead end street ideal for playing all sorts of fantasy games that ended with somebody getting "killed." I particularly remember a little guy named Stuart, who was the king of the dramatic death. Whether pretending to be pierced by an arrow, felled by a bullet or blasted to smithereens by a ray gun, Stuart would run, turn, twist, circle, clutch, groan, shriek, fall, roll, shake and convulse until he had everyone's attention. Then he would "die" and lie perfectly still for several minutes, until one eye would open and look around furtively to see how his performance had been received.

The small hill near our street was Stuart's favorite place to die, for he could reel around the hilltop, reach pleadingly to the sky, and then finally begin his agonized death descent downwards. At the bottom of the hill he would curl into a ball and lay there letting the tragedy of his demise achieve its full affect.

Stuart's death happened almost every day, often several times a day. (Perhaps he was the forerunner of the kid I hear is always getting killed in the *South Park* cartoon on cable television.)

113

Stuart's personal mortality rate climbed to un-heard of peaks on summer days. He liked to be slain, obliterated, murdered, assassinated, wiped out, rubbed out, ambushed, executed, hanged, electrocuted, lethally injected, stabbed, shot, axed, blown up and run over. The only thing he wasn't interested in was a peaceful death.

> *Each of us has been born with wounds, some very visible like Stuart's and others hidden even from ourselves.*

Stuart also had a fierce temper and would get into one fight after another. I can still see his little arms flailing away. Even then, we all had a sense that Stuart was striking out at something (or someone) much larger and more menacing than his friends or imagined enemies.

Stuart had what we used to call a "club foot." I do not hear the phrase used anymore these days. Perhaps advances in surgery have taken care of this birth defect for most kids, at least in this country. But Stuart lived with that deformity and walked and ran with a slight limp, always favoring his crooked foot.

I wonder even today what caused Stuart to invoke daily the trauma of death and to wrap sorrow around himself like a favorite blanket. The throes of Stuart's many deaths found a place in my heart, and as I have grown older—and especially after I began to practice the Cistercian spirituality—the memory of him remains palpable. Each of us has been born with wounds, some very visible like Stuart's and others hidden even from ourselves. We all share the desire for the world to be a good and safe place, even when we know that it is not always so. Perhaps Stuart's dying fantasies were enacted as a way of playing out the enormous mystery into which we are all born and through which we all run...or limp.

Back in New Jersey, fighter jets used to roar overhead as they approached or departed from Mitchell Field, an Air Force base only minutes away. There was a war going on then, but we had no idea of the intimate connection between what was happening above us and Stuart's dramatic demises. We were only playing; we did not know the deep implications of our daily dramas.

We children could not speak of such things, and we adults mostly do not either. The planes still fly overhead, wars still rage around the world, people are still being executed in our name, the poor still die hungry. And on television any given night, more people pretend to die than Stuart would have ever imagined possible.

No one of the old gang is left on that street

now. We all moved to other streets, bringing with us our weaknesses, our limps, our rage, our need for love. I have discovered that the drama that is my own life is born from my own weaknesses. I, too, have had my own episodes of rolling over and playing dead—hoping for a rescue, a dose of sympathy, or at least a drop of attention.

I like to picture Stuart these days, now grown to adulthood, perhaps with his foot miraculously cured, taking a walk on a summer evening with someone he loves. Should they pass two kids fighting on a dead end street, threatening to "kill" each other, I hope Stuart remembers his youthful performances. Perhaps he gently breaks the two kids apart, tells them to shake and make up. Then he takes the arm of the one he loves and they walk slowly, peacefully, quietly toward home, looking up only when a jet roars overhead.

First Things First

It was a sunny morning, and light streamed through the tall windows of my first-grade classroom at Our Lady of Loretto School in Hempstead, New York.

That morning, like every school day morning, Sister Sheila told the class (of what seemed like seventy or eighty six-year-olds!) to stand and exercise. I'm sure this was her way of both getting rid of some of our nervous energy and waking herself up, since she had already been out of bed for four or five hours. (Only since I entered the monastery has the reality of getting up at four or five in the morning occurred to me.)

Sister Sheila stood in the front of the class in full habit and showed us how. "Lift those arms high and stretch, stretch, stretch until you touch the sky," she chirped. So we all lifted our arms and waved them around and tried to touch the sky. "Wiggle your fingers," she called. "Try to tickle the clouds."

David McDonald was my best friend back then, and he sat right in front of me in class. He had a great smile and loved this daily routine. I remember him beaming as he stood and stretched and bowed and twisted each day.

On this particular day, however, David must have forgotten his belt. Or maybe his mom had bought him a new pair of pants that were too large in the waist. In any case, as he tried to touch the sky and tickle the clouds, suddenly his pants fell down straight to his ankles. With something approaching the speed of light, he bent down, grabbed his pants, pulled them up, held them with one hand, and resumed stretching with the other. As I sit here and think about it, I am laughing out loud. It may have been the single funniest thing I have ever witnessed. It was like watching a movie that has been speeded up to the nth degree.

But still his moves were not fast enough. The kids behind us saw what happened, and squeals and laughter filled the room. First-grade girls put their hands to their mouths in utter 1950s Catholic shock. First-grade boys roared in 1950s Catholic delight. David blushed. I froze. Sister Sheila, who had missed the entire thing, shrieked "Siiiiilennncccccce!" (I'm pretty sure that's how the word she yelled is spelled.)

Order was immediately restored, but exercise was over for the day. We all sat down and pulled out our Dick and Jane readers and got back to work—except for an occasional titter from a girl or guffaw from a boy. David remained mortified the rest of the day, but he eventually milked the incident for all the laughs he could get. I'll bet he tells the story to his grandkids.

If there is a choice between touching the heavens and covering our butts, we instinctively will lunge for the latter.

What I remember about that day (in order of importance) are: first, that the funniest things in life are neither planned nor spoken; second, how powerful a single word said with authority and conviction can be; third, how fast we humans can move when caught with our pants down; and fourth, if there is a choice between touching the heavens and covering our butts, we instinctively will lunge for the latter.

Good

She was a waitress in a Shanghai restaurant, and "good" was the only English word she knew. It was a year after the Tianneman Square uprising, when people all over the world watched a horrible confrontation that ended in the slaughter of innocent people by the Chinese government.

I was in China on a tour, and the hesitancy of the Chinese people was obvious. They were afraid to be seen even talking with any foreigner, especially an American. Chinese military men and women seemed to be everywhere, watching every move of tourist and native alike. Our Chinese guides, bona fide members of the Communist party, never once mentioned or even alluded to the Tianneman tragedy. Virtually everyone acted as if it had never happened.

The particular restaurant where the waitress worked was small but busy. She was eager to please but very nervous. She smiled shyly as she approached our table, and our guide spoke with her in Chinese. Then he smiled at us and said, "Just point to what you want from the menu, and she will get it for you." We looked at the menu and saw that there were drawings of ducks, pigs, fish, shrimp, vegetables and other foods. So we pointed out what we wanted.

"Good," she said as the first person in our party ordered. "Good," she said again at the second order, then the next and after each subsequent one. "Good, good, good," she repeated.

I asked our guide if the woman knew any more English, and he fired off something in Chinese to her. She shook her head. "She only knows 'good' and what 'good' means," he replied, missing the irony completely. "Good," I responded.

> **"She only knows 'good' and what 'good' means," he replied, missing the irony completely.**

The food was brought and the waitress hovered within earshot (and finger-pointing shot) lest we want for anything. But we all smiled and ate and drank, nodding to her often and saying "good" several times each. She beamed each time we did so, with a blend of genuine pleasure and relief. "Good," she said, when we finally finished, paid our bill and got up to leave.

There are many things I remember about my trip to China. I was astounded by the vastness of its countryside, the breadth of its history, the throngs of people we saw, the size of its cities, the beauty of its art and architecture. I also remember the fear that hung in the air and the sense that the entire society was being run by a tiny fraction of its huge population.

But the main thing I remember was summed up by that one waitress. To her, everything was "good," and that is a real theological statement— one that fits Cistercian spirituality to a T. It is goodness that humanizes and heals us all, goodness that bridges cultures and politics and menus of any language.

It was Chairman Mao himself who said that one match can ignite a prairie. I believe that some day that waitress's one word, "good," will change the entire world in ways that Mao and his successors never thought possible.

Delivering the Goods

During my summers while in the seminary, one of the jobs I had was delivering beer for Anheuser-Busch. It was not steady work but rather what the union guys called "shape-up." Every morning, fifty or so men (plus one seminarian) would gather in a shed inside the main gate of the Budweiser brewery located on Route 9, just across from Newark International Airport. I was at the low end of the totem pole, but every once in a while I got a job for the day.

The pay was great, I knew my way around the north Jersey area, and I felt like a big shot driving a truck full of beer. One day though, I had trouble finding a street in what the locals call the Down Neck section of Newark. I zigzagged my way up and down a bunch of parallel streets named after American presidents, going under several viaducts that carried commuter train tracks. I carefully noted the signs on each bridge indicating its height to make sure that there was enough room for the truck to pass.

I cannot remember the name of the street where it happened—Garfield? Polk? Bush? Gore?—but whatever street it was must have been recently repaved. For, sure enough, the height was slightly less than the sign indicated, which I discovered the minute the bottom of the bridge tore off the top of the truck.

There's nothing like hitting a bridge to bring a big truck to a dead stop. Another guy was riding with me, and both our heads hit the windshield. We sat there in a mild state of shock, and he turned to me and stated the obvious: "You hit the bridge." With an equal amount of insight, I answered, "I know." It was one of the few statements in my life that I have been absolutely sure of.

A crowd quickly gathered. This was apparently not a first-time experience for them. We climbed out of the truck and looked at the roof, now crumpled like an accordion. Many things went through my mind: the loss of my summer job, having to pay damages, driving through Newark with the truck top sheared off, returning to the brewery and having everyone laugh at me.

Some kid starting letting the air out of the tires, and eventually I was able to ease the truck away from the bridge. I yelled thanks to the kid and he asked for a free case of beer. I told him no, so he gave me the finger and ran off. The crowd began to disperse.

"Better call in," my partner said. So I found a nearby phone and called the dispatcher. He was pretty dispassionate about the whole thing.

"Are you okay?" he asked.

"Yeah," I answered.

"Is your partner okay?"

"Yeah."

"Can you drive the truck?"

"Yeah."

"Was much of the beer ruined?

"Yeah, I mean, no," I answered, not really knowing the true situation. I didn't see anything dripping from the truck, however.

"Well, a little sunshine won't hurt the beer, and those trucks aren't ours anyway," the dispatcher explained. "We rent them, and they'll just give us another one. So get the beer delivered and fill out a form when you get back."

Then he hung up. I felt both relief and dismay. Relief that I wasn't about to be fired and apparently didn't have to pay for the damage. Dismay because I guess I expected some form of expression of personal concern, but all that seemed to matter was getting the beer delivered.

In retrospect, I don't know what I wanted

from the dispatcher. He wasn't about to jump in a car and come comfort me, and I had told him that my partner and I were all right and that the beer was fine. So why shouldn't we deliver the goods?

> *We sat there in a mild state of shock, and he turned to me and stated the obvious: "You hit the bridge."*

And so it was that my partner and I drove the rest of the route with people gawking at the beer truck with no top. When we returned at the end of the day, there were predictable stares and guffaws from a few of our colleagues, but most of them really couldn't have cared less what happened, and probably more than a couple of them had done the same thing once or twice in their careers.

As I look back on my life and all the different routes I have taken, I realize the many mistakes I have made—from miscalculation, from misreading the signs, from worrying too much about what other people thought of me. But there has always been some version of the kid who let the air out of the tires to get me back on the road. (Maybe I should have given him at least one beer.)

The main thing I learned from this episode, however, is not to feel sorry for myself. There are still times when the top of my world seems to be ripped off, but if I look closely I can see that "the goods" are still intact and that a little sunshine won't hurt them. My job is to get back in the truck and deliver them.

So Big

I am one of seven children in my family, and I can remember playing "so big" with my younger sister and brothers when they were babies. You remember the game: You ask a baby how big someone is, and then you hold his or her arms out as wide as you can and say "so big."

"How big is baby?" you ask.

"So big," baby answers.

"How big is Father James?"

"So big."

The game is fun, endless, and works all the time. Babies seem to have a natural and ecstatic response to it. I still play it with every baby I come in contact with. I think babies get the idea that "so big" is as big as things get, that the span of their little arms is the essence of "bigness," that identifying how big things are is a sure way to please the funny adults and older children surrounding them. In their developing minds, the equation goes like this: "so big" = right answer = pleasing the other = laughter, kisses, hugs = let's do it again.

For many of us, however, the definition of

bigness changes as we get older. Big salaries, big cars and homes, big stock portfolios, big jobs, big deals, and big egos become the measure of how right things are in our lives. But there is another way to play this game, and that is to ask, "How big is the heart of God?" The answer, of course, is "so big."

> *In their developing minds, the equation goes like this: "so big" = right answer = pleasing the other = laughter, kisses, hugs = let's do it again.*

I looked about me this morning at our monastery church and the people in it. The monks were there, as well as folks from the area and our overnight visitors. The walls towered above us, light poured through the stained-glass windows, the smell of incense lingered in the air. We were part of a religious tradition that is thousands of years old. It was a living fresco of the human search for God.

But all we know is that we really know very little about God. Maybe we have exhausted the meaning of the very words we use to describe the divine reality, or maybe they never were adequate. Perhaps images for the Godhead no longer have the power and clarity they had in former times. Is God someone we think we shall someday "find" or "comprehend" or "measure" with our seeking? Or is divinity so overwhelming that we simply cannot get our minds and our souls around it?

I think the babies have it right with their game. God's existence and love is far beyond our ability to comprehend. Yet we can continue to stretch our own hearts to the point of breaking in our search, knowing that we will receive nothing but goodness and hugs in return. "So big" is a game we can play over and over and over again without ever tiring of it.

The Lady Who Loved Paperbacks

Before I moved to the monastery, I often sat in my rectory back in Newark and tried to write. There was one woman who used to sit in an old beach chair on the sidewalk in front of her apartment building, and I could see her from my office window almost every day in the warmer seasons. I guessed her to be in her late seventies, and I figured she lived on her social security checks and not much else. On hot days she wore a baseball cap, and on breezy days she had a pretty scarf that kept her wispy hair in place. She always wore a cotton print dress in a lovely shade of one color or another.

What I remember about her is that she loved to read and always had a paperback book with her. Sitting at my computer and stuck on a sentence, I would often gaze out my window and my eyes would invariably come to rest on her. There was something simple and beautiful about the way she read. Every so often she would gently close the book and, with her finger keeping her place, she would raise her head and with a dreamlike smile take in her surroundings. It was as if she had been deeply refreshed from her

135

excursion into the world offered by her book and was bringing the life she had found there onto the street that we shared.

I once saw her in a nearby used bookstore that I frequented. I didn't have the guts to introduce myself, but I peeked at the selection of books she purchased. There were novels by Faulkner, Cather, Welty, Hemingway. I heard her ask the cashier whether a title by the Japanese author Shusaku Endo was ever available. (I made a mental note of the name and later bought several books by that magical writer.)

I wondered what the woman did with the books after she read them. Did she trade them in for other novels? Did she give them away to friends? Was her apartment filled with treasures? Later, I thought of her heart as a treasure house and how she shared her delight in reading with others by the simple fact of reading on the street. When she raised her head from a book that had transformed her, she transformed her own world with her pleasure.

What I learned from the woman who loved paperbacks is that the mystery of being is flowing all around us, both in the imaginary world of literature and in the real world we inhabit. We are in that river and moving with it. She was my river pilot, teaching me the connection between the written word and lived experience.

She and I never exchanged a word, but I think of her every time I write. Wondrous, isn't it, that she gave me something so beautiful, something that I now try to pass on to others?

When she raised her head from a book that had transformed her, she transformed her own world with her pleasure.

I hope, wherever she is today, that her chair is comfortable and the breezes gentle and that she has something good to read. If I could, I would send her my book, with the hope that she might look up from it once or twice and smile.

Creaks

When I was a kid, I shared a room with my twin brother Jimmy on the third floor of one of those big old houses found all over the Northeast. I remember specifically the sound of the heat hissing and banging as it made its way on a winter morning through the basement pipes and upward through the house and finally into the large iron radiator that stood against the wall of our room. Dad used to place water pans behind the radiator to replace the moisture that the heat fried away. Without that water, the air in our room became as dry and arid as any desert's.

That house had a music of its own. Each different door made a unique sound as it opened and closed. The slapping sound of feet on the red linoleum floor in the hall and kitchen softened as someone entered the adjacent carpeted rooms. I can summon the sound of newspaper pages being folded as Dad read them one by one or of change jangling in his pocket when he got up from the couch. The sound of his Zippo lighter flipping open was unmistakable, as was the sound of the switch when he turned on his reading lamp.

In college, there were many nights when I

came home much later than I should have. As I neared the house, I made preparations for as quiet an entry as possible. I took the coins from my pocket and left them on the front seat of the car. I removed the one key I needed for the front door from the key ring, inserted it just right into the lock, and turned it ever so slowly to mute the tell-tale click. Rusty, our dog, would be lying on the rug in the front hall. He would sleepily raise his head, yawn, wag his tail, and get up to investigate. I would pat him on the head, put my finger to my lips, and back down he'd go.

Then I'd start to climb the stairs to the third floor. It took some time—and a few times getting caught—but eventually I got to know every crack and weak spot on those polished wooden stairs. Eventually, I knew exactly where to step and not to step, which slight shifts left or right avoided the tell-tale creaks and allowed a silent ascent to my bedroom. The key was getting past Mom and Dad's bedroom on the second floor. If I could hear snoring from both of them (both of them different sounds, of course), I knew I had it made. My grandmother's room was right near theirs, but I never worried about her because she never squealed. The next morning, she would just give me a knowing look and a wry smile.

It's funny how I can still hear specific sounds even today. I lay awake at the monastery, listening to the creaks and moans of the old buildings, hearing the monks pacing up and down in the hallways, catching the cry of a night owl or the buzzing of an insect, and I remember that old house of my childhood. It was a place full of the sounds of grace.

We get through life by way of our senses. In fact, they are the only way that we can ever come to know God. Through them we touch, hear, smell, taste and see the world around us, the world we have been given as pure gift. Through them we absorb meaning, love, wonder and joy.

> *We get through life by way of our senses. In fact, they are the only way that we can ever come to know God.*

I often wonder if paradise will be a place in which our senses will somehow operate. I hope so. I hope that we will continue to absorb all that is holy and beautiful, slowly and with care, through senses—even if they are different from the five we are used to. The goodness of this life comes to us through our senses. I hope the same is true of the next.

When I die, I'd like to be able to pull out a key to heaven, turn it softly in the lock of the pearly gates, and sneak up the stairs to my loved ones.

Beattie

Her name was Beattie, short for Beatrice, which means "beautiful," and she was. Beattie was in her seventies and was the housekeeper in the rectory I lived in. She had lost her husband many years before and raised their only son to adulthood. She and I got along very well.

Beattie's life was full of many hardships, but she was a real survivor (not like those phony "survivors" I heard about on the television series). She knew how to beautify what little she had. With a nice dress and a new hairdo and a splash of cologne, she was always able to fashion herself with dignity, and no small part of her beauty was the ease with which she shared it with everyone.

Beattie used to go through rough times and needed to talk them out. For some reason she chose me. I would be sitting at the dining room table and could sense that it was a day when she needed to vent. She would come into the house looking a bit down, unload her bag of groceries on the table, and make coffee. Then she would pour two cups and bring them in, sit down across from me, and ask, "Are you busy?" Without awaiting a reply, she would look out the window as if summoning her thoughts from somewhere far away. Then she would turn to me and begin. Usually she would talk non-stop for fifteen or twenty minutes, going over what was by then mostly familiar terrain: losing her husband early, being ignored by her friends, being verbally abused by someone at the grocery store, the many failures of her legendary car.

> *All our "conversations" ever seemed to do was confirm her firmly held conviction that things never change one little bit.*

I would listen and nod, occasionally looking out the window to see how many more words were gathered on the horizon. Then I would glance back at Beattie, who was by then near tears, and just smile, hoping that something she might see in me or something I might say would help. All our "conversations" ever seemed to do was confirm her firmly held conviction that things never change one little bit.

Finally, though, she would finish, wipe her eyes, blow her nose, and say, "Thank you, Father. You're a nice boy." The amazing thing was that she then appeared to be fine, even aglow, for much of the rest of the day and into the next.

Beattie passed away a few years ago. I do

not think that any of her problems were ever really solved. They just piled up until they got too high, then she found someone on whom to unload them, and then they lost their claim on her spirit.

I learned from Beattie that few things in life ever really change. Yet the talking out of our hurts to someone who will listen transforms them into something more tolerable. It's like the burdens of living become lighter just by sharing them.

Even though I've now taken the vow of silence, there are still times when I find a friend, pour him or her a proverbial cup of coffee, and say, "Are you busy?" And, bless Beattie's heart, it always seems to help. Words do many things, and at least one of those things is magical: Words build living bridges across which we humans meet and heal one another.

The Coney Island Pub

In the west of Ireland, near Bushtown in Glenamaddy, is a large field, and in the middle of that field is the Coney Island Pub. I went there many years ago, and I learned something about myself.

I was with another Irish-American friend (the name Behrens is German, although my mother's a Sullivan) who had some cousins he had never met in Ireland, and one evening we drove through many small towns to get to the pub to meet them. Finally, we turned onto the last dirt road that was on the pencil-drawn map we had been given. We couldn't see anything at first except the field, but as we drove a little further we came across a sign that had an arrow and the words "To the C. I. Pub: Approach with Care."

So we turned onto the field itself, and sure enough we discovered that there was something that passed for a road beneath the wheels of the car, although it was really only where the grass had been matted down by cars that had passed before us. We soon came upon an odd-looking building that we couldn't see from the road. It was built like a bunker—close to the ground and seemingly impenetrable. There was one door and a few windows, all of them open and streaming light from the inside. Several cars—which we had also not seen—were parked outside. The whole thing reminded me of the vanishing land in the musical *Brigadoon.*

As we got out of our car, we heard laughter and singing coming from the pub. It was a delightful sound, almost magical in quality. Little did I know that the magic was only about to begin. All around us the Irish sky was turning a rich red with the setting of the sun. The lush greens and browns of the field were speckled with gold as the sun's rays played off the moisture from an afternoon shower that clung to every leaf, weed and blade of grass. If there were ever a night and a place that could entice me to believe in the legendary Irish myths, it would be that night around the Coney Island Pub.

We walked through the door and found a room filled with people. They all looked up. A few waved or smiled at us, and some raised their mugs of beer in welcome. A haze of cigarette smoke drifted in the air, one long wisp slowly drifting beneath the single large light fixture on the ceiling. The room was hot, but not uncomfortably so, and my companion and I sat at an empty table.

There didn't seem to be any kind of waiter or even a traditional bar, but we soon spotted a hole in the wall through which an arm would periodically emerge with a bottle of beer that one of the customers would grab. A young man came over to us and said, "You must be the Americans. Paddy is waiting to welcome you in the back room." He nodded in the direction of the hole in the wall. There, behind a table of especially boisterous men, we spotted a door that was slightly ajar. We peeked in and saw the proprietor with three other men, who turned out to be my friend's distant cousins, sitting around a small table. Smiles lit all their faces as we tentatively entered the back room, and they made space for the two of us at the crowded table. We all introduced ourselves around, and Paddy brought out beers for everyone. He beamed at the opportunity to host a first meeting of blood relatives in his establishment.

I was the odd man out, but I felt at home with these men, who like the apostle Nathaniel, were "without guile." It occurred to me as I sat there that I had not been treated like a stranger once while in Ireland—a land in which I knew absolutely no one before I arrived. It seems that the Irish have a natural instinct for healing human estrangement. Ireland is a place of openness: open faces and smiles, open doors and windows, open souls to God's grace (which I think they would define as whatever God brings).

My friend and I chatted for a while about

our trip, our respective homes and families, what we each knew about our Irish ancestry (which wasn't much). The men knew that we were both priests, and I had the feeling that this knowledge put a slight restraint on where the conversation might have gone, but I considered this to be a sign of respect for the Church and their religious heritage.

> *It is the patrons of Paddy's pub who have given me the permission and the courage to write, to put out who and what I am before others, to trust that my words will be accepted for what they are–no more and no less.*

"Well," said Paddy (and that was his real name, I wouldn't make that up), "The fun is about to begin. Come with me." We followed him and the others into the larger room. Everyone was now sitting in a circle three to five people deep. There was a lone, straight-backed chair in the center of the circle, directly beneath the one light fixture, still swirling with smoke. Honest to God, it looked like something out of an old Humphrey Bogart movie.

Seats of honor had been reserved for us, and soon a young woman stood up and walked slowly to the chair in the center. She stopped right in front of the chair, looked around at the group with a gaze that showed not a bit of fear or self-consciousness, fixed a wisp of her hair with her hand, smiled and then started to sing. Her voice was the closest I have ever heard to that of an angel. She sang a sad Irish song about a boy who went away and never returned. She easily convinced me that she was singing with a heart broken by the loss of her own true love. When she finished, applause and cheers filled the room, and a feeling of love did too. She bowed and took her seat again.

A young man got up from his seat and went to the center chair. He too looked around and smiled with confidence. He sang a song about a young woman's beauty—her hair, her eyes, her lips and how she used them. He finished and bowed to the same applause and cheering as the woman had received.

Thus it went as the night wore on. Different people did different things. Some sang, some told stories, others told jokes. One man got up and spoke very matter-of-factly about a miracle he had experienced: The Blessed Mother had spoken to him in a dream. A hush fell over the room as he spoke, and after he finished the applause was different—more reverential than anything else, and certainly without a hint of doubt or derision.

Near the end of the evening, Paddy leaned over and asked me if I had a song or a story to share. I sheepishly declined. He told me that some day I would be ready to share what and who I am. He winked as he said it. It was a "you wait and see" kind of wink.

And that's what I learned that night. After "waiting and seeing" for many years, I realize that Paddy was right. How I wish I had been free enough, confident enough, centered enough, to get up and share a piece of myself with those wonderful people at the Coney Island Pub. They would not have judged me. They would have accepted me as one of them, just as they accepted everyone else that night. It is the patrons of Paddy's pub who have given me the permission and the courage to write, to put out who and what I am before others, to trust that my words will be accepted for what they are—no more and no less.

As my friend and I drove away from the pub and onto the road, there was another sign: "Leave with Gratitude and Care." I certainly did.

Conclusion

I was in bed last evening waiting for sleep to come. There was a full moon, and its light poured into my room like a soft, silver glow. I lay there thinking about the day's activities, not focusing on anything particular.

Then the past came flooding into my mind, as it does many nights here in Conyers. The memories of all the grace I have experienced in my life started to warm me, and I began to wonder if the memories themselves are a form of prayer.

I thought back to the night my father was dying and my mother and brothers and sisters and I were all there in the hospital room. I remember feeling a similar warmth. The day before, Dad had asked me how he would know how to find—"on the other side"—my twin brother Jimmy, who had died in a car accident when we were both teenagers. I said that Jimmy would come and find him.

I remember Dad crying years ago when he asked me to help him pick out what Jimmy should wear when he was buried. But I remember other things, too, like the time Jimmy and I were in early high school and Dad brought us to New York to buy our first suits. Then he took us to his office on Fifth Avenue and introduced us to the people with whom he worked. I remember how proud he was of us and how proud we were of him.

Jimmy died long ago, but I still dream about him often. I have heard that means there is some sort of unfinished business between us, and I'm sure that is true. Maybe that is partly why I took his name when I entered the monastery.

After I finally fell asleep last night, I dreamed that Jimmy and I went to Europe. I didn't have a valid passport, but Jimmy smiled and said not to worry. It all seemed so natural. He is always young when I dream of him, nor do I realize in my dreams that he is dead. I want to say to him, "Jimmy, my story is your story. My memories are your memories."

Acknowledgments

"If you want to play outside then first spend time inside the house and write those thank-you notes," said my mom many times, many years ago. And so I wrote and then I played. But as the years passed I came to enjoy the writing as much as the playing. So I thank Mom for making me write first and play later. Now, here in the "later," I also thank:

—My editor, Greg Pierce, and everyone at ACTA Publications, and the staffs at the *National Catholic Reporter, Living Faith, St. Anthony Messenger, The Liguorian, Notre Dame Magazine, Spirit and Life* and other publications, who have helped me shape and share my words.

—Those whose love and encouragement moved me to think something good was at play in my writing: Mary Dwyer (my godmother), Joan Chittister, OSB, Dolores Leckey, Dick Liddy, Archbishop Peter Leo Gerety, Bernard Johnson, OCSO, Andre Dubus, Walker Percy, John Monczunski, Anne Lamott, Karen Leibnitz and John Arnold, Michael Farrell, Teresa Malcolm, Tom Fox, John Allen, Francis Michael Stiteler, OCSO, Patrick Hart, OCSO, Damian Turk, OCSO, Patrick Samway, SJ, Mark Neilsen, Ward Moore,

Frank Goss, Joe and Anita Puglisi, Susan McBride, Valerie O'Reilly, Pat Ryan, Peggy and Walt Bomhoff, Fredrick Gartner, our new abbot, Basil Pennington, and all my brother monks here at Conyers.

—Those whose lives generously offer the beauty that is grace to written words: PeeWee McCollum, J.P. McIsaac, Beatrice Palperio, Anna Sullivan, Jean and Carl Kalemba, Steve and Claire Filipow, Emmanuel Capozzelli, Geralyn Barnett, Steve and Anne Barron.

There are more. You know who you are. I thank you, too.

ALSO AVAILABLE

Grace Is Everywhere
Reflections of an Aspiring Monk
James Stephen Behrens, OCSO
with a Foreword by Dolores Leckey
and an Afterword by Joan Chittister, OSB

Best-selling vignettes from the author's life at the Monastery of the Holy Spirit in Conyers, Georgia, with reflections on the connection between monastic spirituality and daily life. (160-page paperback, $9.95)

Be Gentle, Be Faithful
Daily Meditations for Busy Christians
James Stephen Behrens, OCSO

A page-a-day reflection for each day of the year. Each meditation is illuminated by a carefully chosen Scripture verse. Not tied to a specific calendar year. (366-page paperback, $9.95).

Seasons of Grace
Reflections from the Cloister
Gail Fitzpatrick, OCSO
with a Foreword by Kathleen Norris

Fifty reflections, each begun with a Bible quote and ended with an original prayer, that follow both the seasons of the year and the liturgical seasons. The first book by Mother Gail, the well-respected abbess of Our Lady of the Mississippi Abbey in Dubuque, Iowa. (192-page paperback, $9.95)

**Available from booksellers
or call 800-397-2282 in the U.S. or Canada.**